KINGDOM COME RADIO SHOW

Joni Wallace

KINGDOM COME RADIO SHOW

Joni Wallace

Cover design by Robert Drummond

Published 2016 by Barrow Street, Inc.
(501) (c) (3) corporation. All contributions are tax deductible.
Distributed by:
    Barrow Street Books
    P.O. Box 1558
    Kingston, RI 02881

Barrow Street Books are also distributed by Small Press Distribution,
SPD, 1341 Seventh Street Berkeley, CA 94710-1409, spd@spdbooks.org;
(510) 524-1668, (800) 869-7553 (Toll-free within the US); amazon.com;
Ingram Periodicals Inc., 1240 Heil Quaker Blvd, PO Box 7000,
La Vergne, TN 37086-700 (615) 213-3574; and Armadillo & Co., 7310
S. La Cienega Blvd, Inglewood, CA 90302, (310) 693-6061.

Special thanks to the University of Rhode Island English Department and
especially the PhD Program in English, 60 Upper College Road, Swan
114, Kingston, RI 02881, (401) 874-5931, which provides valuable
in-kind support, including graduate and undergraduate interns.

First Edition

Library of Congress Control Number: 2016951767

ISBN 978-0-9973184-1-8

CONTENTS

ONE

TWO

THREE

FOUR

ONE

Twilight amphitheater

To pan the sky over this city is to speak a stunning nothing. In the mind's eye, an approaching storm formation as atomic cloud gathered over Trinity Site, 1945.

A physicist's exhalation of relief/joy/fear inside it, a gathering of mule deer underneath.

Because there are recordings of J. Robert Oppenheimer speaking under this same expanse, in this same terrain, some part of the man, a history, seems forever caught in the pines, the blades of grass.

If I touch the trees, his voice comes alive there.

If I touch the grass, I can just make another, Hank Williams, twang inside my own personal childhood pastoral.

Sometimes the sky formation morphs, crepuscular rays reaching through the cumuli and onto the sweep, cinematic, projector-lit: a western.

Oppenheimer pacing a narrow room in cool of evening. Smoke from a cigarette leaked all around him. His mind working the equation that says the atmosphere will/ will not ignite when the gadget blows straight up into Kingdom Come.

For the tilt shot, Kitty Puening Oppenheimer, drink in hand, the *clink*, *clink* of ice against glass. Outside a window, caw and call of magpies, a scuffling in the aspen grove.

Cut to a long drive on a stretch of road, almost-dark, the percussive hiss of cicadas in stereo. Hank singing AM, *On this road of sin you are sorrow bound.* Lines I heard from the backseat of a Mercury station wagon somewhere between Las Cruces and Los Angeles, highway to anywhere, USA.

I am simply opening the record. Every cut is a lie. These shots were never next to each other in time this way.

To render the landscape is to find the voices there, to add and absent them, to attach my own to them, a mapping.

Cartography of sotto voce. Temporally stitched together by birds, by deer, by the animation of insects.

For the dossier, primeval forest below a wide-open gala.

Einsteinian dimensions.
Prodigal self, an other, set to witness.
This listening.

For the sound track, *scree* of a raptor.

You are here marks the spot where the deer lay down under blue immensity.

render *v.* 1: to depict; 2: to make or create a thing received in alternative media; 3: to transmit; to receive. From Latin, *reddo*, to give, return.

Inside Dance Music, Outside Night Music

The lodge production plays.
Part where woodlands haunt, part where aspen glow,
part where America, part where we liked to get smashed.

Welcome, says Oppenheimer, night watchman.

His incomprehensible footfall because no foot at all.

One evening I looked up from the sink stand, he says.
Twin albino fawns there.
Mute masterpiece, statistically speaking.

Text for the creature case.

I place it there, an understanding.

Sometimes I think I step inside his head.
Sometimes I find the things caught there
catch also within my visible.

Oppenheimer Drive

1.

Here in the Atomic City, shape of a pedal bone on the Jemez.
Here my house (my mother's, my father's) beside the canyon,
a stable, an Appaloosa on which to ride.
One history as cacophony, hoofbeats across a mesa.
One's own as illusory, a street or field, scatter of mule deer
glimpsed at dusk.

***

The first water tower says *snow*, the second, *more snow*.
Across the hill, menagerie of deer, furs
strewn out.
Inside the clouds their breaths make, bitty lightning,
scent of deader grass. Leaves.
When they dream, they dream in tinder trunks,
maybe *shzzzzzzz* of a Zamboni scraping ice.
Maybe a blaze, murmur of low planes,
a helicopter-strung Bambi Bucket of slurry.

How does it go, the deer medley?

Soft glow of a salt lick.
Above the deer fence, place where
a stag leaps and seems to catch,
midair.

***

Wind shimmer where a man, Oppenheimer,
is learning his job description
called Shadow Puppeteer.

I can trace the dark and the light, forms in the theater.

Lub dub, a sigh.

December moon, a body.
To light the ready-made.
Our dumb and deaf projection.
The moniker "Everyday Life."
When we walk home together,
I hear the wind's exquisite things,
wormholes and worms, the secret of fawns,
mouse intervals, arias, a clearing.

***

When the deer leaped   I saw
When the deer leaped   ruby orbits
When the deer leaped   chunks of ice
When the deer leaped   a path
When the deer leaped   x
                              a jack
                              memory mark

2.

See how twilight makes its game,
hat/rabbit hat/rabbit chattering off.

Swag of deer in head-to-tail formation.

If I open the curtain, cutting room where one
sits and sits some more.

If I am *metteur en scène*, fly sheet on the table,
invisible-ink pen to ink in the ghost particles,
sinkers on the trinket tray.
(All the way to China.)

If I am cinematographer, standstill, these skies.
A silver screen, *Uranium Drive-In*.

If I am audiographer, *boom, boom* says the boom carpet.
If I am oneirographer, beginning-, middle-, end-deer,
a threnody.

Enter deer tagged U-235, a smasher, *rye whiskey, a cry*.
Enter deer made of light (star of light emitted just here).
Enter deer with a window for a side (lilies, a bone-white plexus).

And enters Oppenheimer (he sees his decent suit).
Within the image library, an oh of surprise and sound like no legs,
no tail, a hush across and never touching a dance floor.
Hello you and you and you in your flammable coats, says he.

***

In 't Hooft's rendition of unseeable,
one can walk right through a flickering herd
into a kind of reversible spell.
Any number of constellated points,
tinseled or aureoled, a tuning along
the vapor of deer.
And opens into a theater, hum or hymn.
Forest, Sky, Melody, Harmony.
Song I sang as a child.
Reverse the spell, and woods,
a thicket, reassemble.
Into a room so bright.
The forest presentation of *Come in, little match.*

If I put my hand through, twenty-seven bones.
If I put a foot, twenty-six.
Bone testament.
So when I sing.
I am he/she, am I?
I am the bird, am I?
Follow the string.

3.

When the canna grew, red and waxy,
in the contamination zone, some said
ears of erased things.

An aural architecture.

Dear grief-black rain, said the parapet shadows.
A Torii gate, mouth agape.

The deafening matutinal ringing.

Where eyes meet.

Blare. A blare.

***

In the back of a retina, cryptochrome.

(This part of the frame occupied by birds.)

Detail of a halo, one thousand suns.

It makes a distortion bow.

No direction home, warbles a stone.

Earth's chorus in the far-off firmament.

Cranes queued up in a boreal marsh. Ionizing ash.

4.

Space and time, August 10, 1945.

Stitch-stitch of the train's black shoe.

A man, Yamahata, entering Nagasaki.

His task set forth.

To document.

Black of a camera.

Clicks of a shutterfly until it sticks

to open, black endless.

When Yamahata names the exposure, he names it

And then I put my hands through my face.

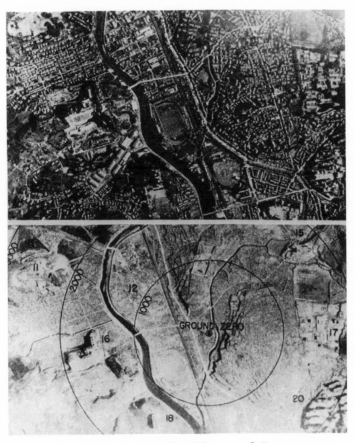

Nagasaki, Japan, post-strike. Library of Congress.

5.

The likeness for desolation is drawn partly
with breath, small and low, partly with mind.

Partly with flying days, all action, crash-up's
dead-drop in a winter still.

I dress for the part, white shoes, white dress.
I place my porcelains along the white ground.

At gloom hours, a dread piece playing the walls,
zed in lo-fi.
A rhapsody of teeth, 0.0-1.3.3/3.1.3.
My beautiful toothy darling, it swirls.

For such thing as perfectly bleating.
Now the timbre of silver-white trees.
Dapples.
The wound-let *I* s.

In the center of the city on the hill,
a boy, his startle-pattern dog, on a field.
Blake tattooed on an arm.
The words *Live Right. Do No Harm.*
The boy kicking it off outside the high school auditorium.
I wasn't going anywhere in this town.
Anywhere, anywhere, I wasn't going,
he thinks this,
then *come up you witchy combination.*
Which ends in E.
E for Elks Club.
E for Everyone in the Antler Room, applause, applause,
Oppenheimer, Kitty, everyone below chandelier lights like the
whole star lot.

God-ish, they say,

the *plink plink* configuration.

Across the way, Oppenheimer Drive,
ticker marquee I'm under.
Snow making dot-to-dots on a doe's back.
The scene so freaking gorgeous.
My tint pick exactly.

Documentary in which Oppenheimer Both Acts and Directs

In the photograph, your chair, your face, on the mesa,
1946/*You can't see a ghost, it's only light fissures on film*

What kind of light is that, technically speaking?/*Dead*

A resemblance to script, fragment/*Nothing but*
What I want to show: a day's remains/*sage*

How a flock makes a flare/*rib cage of not*

Black/blond of a raccoon in the road/*Ghostland*

Documentary with Kitty and Dramatic Representation of Snowfall

For the Super 8 propaganda piece,
Kitty skates the rink below Omega Bridge.
Fur coat, pillbox hat, her muffling muff.
Mister F-B-I man, she mutters, mostly inaudible
as she glides past the figure, uniformed form
in a hockey box.
Because the celluloid degrades just there,
a part that seems mostly shine,
scrape of metal blades over ice, a glare view
into which her loveliest stunt unfolds.
The one where her coat breaks
into rabbits, a hundred kits dropped
onto ice, blizzard of down
in the sleight of a flurry, then flash
where the filmstrip breaks into
bright.

Starlings Pirouette from Fence Posts, Diggers and Spades

An entire story.

Its entirety: *Look at me, ruin.*

Deer, Detail

https://soundcloud.com/kingdomcomeradioshow/deer-detail

TWO

The forest face, fox-shaped leaves

Sometimes a moment placed inside a document makes a surface so that what lies under it breathes a little, even absents that space and makes a surprise, later, like downdraft in a box canyon, a sudden litter of foxes under brush. For the series, zigzag of tracks out from a thicket. *V* of clabbering geese overhead. Copse architecture of symmetry, disruption.

document *v.* 1: to make a piece of written, printed or electronic matter that provides information or evidence; 2: to record or capture a place, person or event to use as evidence or proof. From Latin, *documentum*, example, proof, lesson.

Spy After Spy, a Shimmy

What makes us wake and walk out
of the house into the thrum of what
has hummed all around us in sleep,
fluted or felled?

Buzz of an engine, more observable bees.
A woodpecker, speckled and flecked, its
tap-tap above a rooftop.

I'm trying to capture a memory,
one moment on a porch, an echo-fragment
where a jet makes its speed sonic,
sidereal report perfectly timed
for my sister and me, decoy spies
in a summer of spies and I am falling

the most elegant fall, she a drape, legs,
an arm, one white Mary Jane kicked
so high it catches, and caught, jars metalmarks
from branches, an eclipse of yellow, orange
camouflage loosed, our contretemps.

For the still shot, straight up through
a pine, tat of a cirrus.

Mole code for the sleeper shoe.

Nostalgia is the insect ringing.
Repeat, repeat, molecule manifesto
on a wing splotch.

Mesas and Particles

Some nights inside the caterwaul of coyotes
the telephone rings, very late or very early.
My father walks out into darkness.
My mother still sleeping
and I am.
He drives along the road, surreal
in the animal-hours, turns,
drives past a gun tower, past a guard station,
up a hill, another turn and another hill and then
far out across a mesa to a concrete building
where one mile of nothing whispers by.
My father works the machine that makes the mile go past,
invisible flowering.
Some mornings I dream the machine itself is invisible.
There is my father fixing the invisible machine.
He can see through it and I can see
through the thought of it into the azure wave
of morning, wave the color of an iris inside an iris.
Look, he says, *no hands.*

My Flashlight Shines on a Deer

From where I stand under the pink

moon, the woods seem incandescent,

color of other-worldly.

It's September.

(*nails, ball bearings, a screw*)

I make an O where my daughter

left a pink plastic polka-dot fawn

out on a bed of Easter grass.

The Decemberists playing on my iPod.

(*everyone face-down on floor again*)

Beauty, melancholy, beauty.

For the outro, the *stut stut* stutter of fireflies,

(*tiny shrapnel*) makeshift twinkles.

How it feels stroboscopic.

Static of punctures.

What has no home turns, comes

toward me, bioluminescent sequence

on a sylvan scrim.

Wolf Project with Fear of Wolves

1.

Because all of it is an assemblage of sound, I can turn the volume up to where everything is a kind of scream. Violinings of crickets, canned sounds of flies, the perfect glistening of ice on the wolf-studded stage. Someone's interior *shushshush* murmuring inside a heart or rush from an amygdala. Weed-fires. The wolves should bare their teeth. Should stoke the flames and sharp their eyes for a game of cup-and-ball. *Your baby or mine?* I ask. A woman in the front row answering *Stardust, lady,* I think, I can't be sure.

2.

Maybe we shouldn't say the part where the wolves come back and we watch from rooftops. All the wires, worry-wires. Each heating a sock of air.

The word we didn't know was cull *n.* 1: a saxophone playing voices of children laid down in the birches.

The word we didn't know was pelage *n.* 1: a metallic taste in the mouth; 2: *thwack,* the sound of, as in scythes.

Little wolf outside the kitchen, slink of a pelt under eaves, the theory of wolves is broken. So difficult to discern the deer, some dressed as wolves, some simply as twists, some hooks.

3.

Arroyos. Astonishing skies. These for the coda, end scene where wolfpack leaps into glass. My blues, someone else's browns or hazels, looking back at them through branches. Sleet-fall, wolf bodies illumined by what seems video glow. Now we hear what the wolves hear, a mouse scratching *possum, possum,* hum of a cold front. *Dear creatures,* we say into the whine of a cell-phone tower. How we love the cage. Glint of bars and a silvery view.

4.

Temps mort:

Come away with me, voices a she-wolf.

Moths float in.

Thorax, an abdomen.

Stipples and stripes.

So beautiful.

It was.

Documentary with Sea, a Weeping (Fukushima, 2011)

1.

What the eye gathers.

Antler chandeliers hung from metal girders. Surf behind.
A belt of radiographic bodies projected out from under
a reactor core.

2.

What the eye gathers.

Plum dawn. Deer at swim, plimsolls up, a synchronicity
of antlers in the offing off a strait off Russia. One blinking

    there may never be a snake

another,

    what on earth for dousing the sea?

3.

What the eye gathers.

Green-glass bobber on a shoreline. Bottles, schema. A scrawled drawing of ginkgos, cedars, a map of Nara. In a graphic depiction, sika deer wading through X-ray light. Inside each deer, various shades of red: safflower, madder, vermillion, carmine, imperial, ruby, crimson. The inked character for *brilliant light, boom.*

4.

What the eye gathers.

Decay, exploded view: deer smacking heads, deer bodies, deer scavengers, deer bloat, deer autolysis, deer putrefaction, deer blow-flies, deer vapors, deer skeletons, deer carbon, deer particles, deer photons, deer axions, deer dark matter. This as translation error, looping.

5.

What the eye gathers.

Symphony of deer on a beach.
Moon jellies beyond, a bloom of, the chemical blush
of filaments inside globes.
Roils and rollers.
Gulls to roll over a changeover.
A drone flies into the drizzle.
Another.
Disaster protocol.

All the Buffalo Once Were Deer (for L)

Fawns line up in flinty rows.
Charcoal-ecru spots, thundercloud-dusty-cloudy
spots, slate-resplendent-silver spots.
They make clever hoof patterns, kick-pleats kicked
into sides of dust devils, hoofprint intaglios
in particulate patterns.
Sun as jackhammer hammering *no-shade-ever.*
Inside the buzz of mowers, whispered names
for Velvets, *Anonymous, Secret Stag,*
toe-taps for the gone-befores, a matter of math.
Deer Do Tricks signs the sign.
Foreknow, I think, my dreaming baby girl
dreaming baby-deer dreams, pellets
and sugar cubes, landscape from above,
arc of deer on the checkerboard.
For the encore, cloud busts.
Ark sequence.
Pause and then beast parade,
shags, great heads, a saunter or a canter
across new and viridescent plains.

Big Sky Is a Country

We arrive to a small unpretty picnic,
animal opera played over prairie,
the fawn limned over a power line.
Raptor drop
in the leggy shape of dangle.
From the cadaver of a no-scent fawn, deer effluvia.
The swoon or simply knockout of a synchronized sacking.

King Stone.
He took the light rail, man,
straight out to nowhere,

laments the voice-over,
then *Do not let the children see*
says no one in particular,
and *goddamn it* or *holy shit,*
this for the helpless impulse the audience feels
while the movie keeps going over tragic.

Interlude of rain, rivers and streaks
miles out, grist for the poets, composers,
measuring.

Pylon shadows in sutured rows.
Hawk floating in on a thermal of sheer.

Documentary with Kitty and Fire Show

1.

In the face of roar, her face is lamb. For fixed-wings, the spotters, those that fly in, a neon face, flamingos or *fabulous Las Vegas* blinked through a billow of smoke. Jumpers target the crown fires, parachute skirts blooming over smoke-top. *How I've gone wrong,* Kitty thinks, drunk-thought with bubbly and rapt at the Shelter Show. A torch song paints her visage.

2.

Insert Starlight Hotel, Galaxy Lounge. The steel sheen of a fire door behind the barkeep, B-side to an alley. Reflected thereon, a single planet. Oblivion Dial. *Open it,* says what she thinks she hears. Hears again.

3.

She does. On a backdrop, Holy Trinity in cartoon, three painted flames in convection haze, an incendiary omnipresence on the high alpine skeletal set. When steps into kliegs, Roadrunner. Coyote. Cartoon bomb on legs. *Crinkle crinkle crinkle* goes a zephyr goes the spectacle parade.

Interior with Oppenheimer and Cranes

Anatomy

        chinks

of pneumatic

        hollows sacs of air

slight slush of marrow

        says Oppenheimer

end pin on a scapular

        this comes in

muted, red-crowned

        uneven

susurrations

        disturbed over wire

of an unstable nucleus

        a frequency

100 million electron volts

        no flesh to seal it

hurtling

        trumpet flourish

elliptical swoop

        red-crowned

electrostatic

        now do you know where we are

visual grainy

Mock-up for a Century

So many versions. I stack them, a vision box, diorama where I
am tracking small game. Greyhounds, rabbit-rags, a bus depot's
I am leaving, concertina shine, the dog version of *we love you,*
yeah, yeah, a covey of grouse, weasel curling into a drainpipe.
Over red-clay hills, pockets of juniper, landfills filled with this
or that blight, the comfort-me junk. A billboard, Miss Atomic
Test, 1954, neon signage for *Atomic Lounge, Electron Café,*

fallout-shelter propaganda.   When the gathering
is done, I add insomnia, a braid of heat. Wasps to fly in and
speak their tongues.

Sky Piece

THREE

ion of a fission or thermonuclear bomb produces

stimulate the reaction of atomic nuclei of the

an ignition point exists and is surpassed, the

be propagated to all parts of the atmosphere.

of the reaction demands that the energy product

ion exceed the losses from that region. The en

f the kinetic energy of particles which are prod

tions. The product particles, through collision

A man night-walking, his hand inside the big hand of death

What is that hush I hear all around me? Oppenheimer was heard to be muttering. In periods of dread he suffered a kind of hyperacusis, so that even the steps of a doe at evening made a *clip-clop* so loud he got no sleep. Sometimes he rose in those small hours and played recordings of Bach, Prokofiev, Ravel, Glière. This made the room seem most like moonlight on woods. A place he could sleep inside. When I awaken in these same small hours, what I document seems most like deer glimpsed through timber.

Jackrabbit and Black Hole

(For Radio)(Voice of Oppenheimer)

See how the mind links a landscape?
Mesa, concrete block, a turtle turned upside down.

From my robin's–egg blue convertible,
a windshield of daisies made a chain.

Assemblage for the Nation Play, the exact
placement of thunderheads no accident.

I saw a jackrabbit, hump under celadon sage.
I saw a jackrabbit, bas-relief, meat-mark

in the bleak terrain.
I saw the panorama take no pictures.

I saw the dream object, a great mantel eye,
incandescent brain loosed high above desert tableau.

I saw breaking from the body, sun.
I saw breaking from the sun, false dawn,

zinnias, flash which bloweth, ruptured
flies, mortal flesh of the hare, then
throat upon throat upon throat

whoosh

I wear I wear it some more.

Broadcast for Kitty with Sparkle and Fade
(For Radio)(Voice of America)

Exosphere, themosphere, troposphere,
a holographic display.
Pinpoints of planets, semaphore stars above.
Closer in, B-17s, B-29s,
fetishistic miniature pilots before exquisite controls,
a tear-shaped bomb.
We are far out over sea/we are close in over target,
gazetteers a black box.
Projected mushroom cloud as backdrop.
In the seat next to her, indentation of a small
cat, its vintage purr into
the scratch track, *Too blue to cry.*
Chirps of one kind or another start up,
details to be sorted in telegraphs
(she becomes the docent, she becomes
the room, she becomes the color, she becomes
the document.)

Pine Piece

(For radio) (Voice of Oppenheimer [just at audibility])

The
body
decays.
Yellow cake
decays. Give a listen.
Hardscrabble in the dayroom.
Murders of crows, huddles of rats.
One million shovels and powder to tell:
fingerprints, whorls on a pane, shame-plates
and pies. If I tell you the way repetition soothes an
ache. If I tell you crows streak past buildings, scavengers
on the draft, stark as spears in a cadence above the mesa.
Say it. World made of stories. Not atoms.
My indigo
composition.
Half-life,
a phrase.

How Mercurial, the Water Tower (after Meret Oppenheim)

(For Radio)(Voice of Oppenheimer [O]; Voice of Oppenheim; Insect Chorus)

O: Day after day, the water tower, sentinel.
It casts a pall amidst the praise-chorus, glittering strange.

CHORUS: (sound of cicadas)

OPPENHEIM: Acclaim, éclat.
For the sake of.

O: It makes my ghastly ladder.

Chorus: *tick tick tick tick*

O: The eulogy plays.

CHORUS: (sound of cicadas)

O: If I climb up into the hollow,
another, bell of a bomblet.

OPPENHEIM: KILROY WAS HERE graffitied on the casing.

O: Text for the boneyard.

OPPENHEIM: Theater of many.

O: The matter of Mother. Her white-gloved hand.

OPPENHEIM: Kidskin, the glove.

O: I paint myself in.

OPPENHEIM: Red ganglion. Ventricular boughs.

CHORUS: (fades to silent)

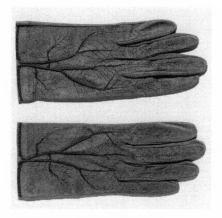

Meret Oppenheim, *Glove*
(Image credit, p. 81)

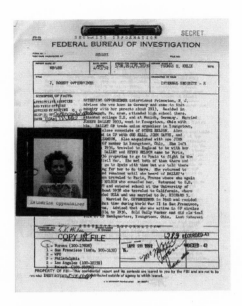

Sonnet for Kitty

(For radio)(Voice of Oppenheimer [O]; Voice of Kitty Oppenheimer [Kitty])

O: Be sure your tongue is sharp
Kitty: Said the cock, crowing

***

O: Be sure to hold your tongue
Kitty: Said the bell, tolling

***

O: Queen Cloche of a Sparrow
Kitty: My transparent crown

***

O: King Caught-in-a-Flock
Kitty: Half-withered, a limb

***

O: Grandiloquent nature
Kitty: Our apocryphal scarecrow

***

O: This matter of numbers—
Kitty: Vault of stars

***

O: When the boatman calls
Kitty: Look back at the mountains

Remains, Mountains, Rivers (Japan, 1960)
(For Radio)(Voice of Oppenheimer)

When I came upon the layer of raptors,
I did not know the skeleton grotto.

When I came upon the layer of foxes,
I did not know the sediment soil.

When I came upon the layer of stone,
I did not know the refuge of illusion.

When I came upon the hive,
I did not know the force of the fury.

When I came across the sea,
I did not know the listening bilge.

I feel no worse tonight than last.
Come close, my secrets leak,

sometimes harmonic, sometimes irregular,
lean in, at ground we meet,

a melody escapes my ear—

(Music begins to play, Beethoven's String Quartet in C Minor)

I Am Oppenheimer

(For radio)(Voice of Oppenheimer [O]; Voice of Issui Yoshida [Poet])

O: The film goes silent, canyon lit by tracers,

smoke petals, a braille of "loves me, loves me not."

POET: *Time's bell.*

O: My dossier drawn into dust on the Cadillac hood,

WASH ME.

POET: *On the roof, a bird's nest is beginning to crumble.*

O: An equation etched on a headstone.

POET: *I weigh, before me, my own skull.*

O: I sleep well, quicksilver inside the hooves

of a silver-gray horse.

POET: *Words.*

O: I sleep well in the matchbox I call Theater of Null.

POET: *Shadowless vault.*

OPPENHEIMER: I sleep well inside an atom I call Manhattan.

POET: *Phantom of enormous structure.*

O: Work long done, I lodge inside the guts of a mouse.

POET: *Thorns.*

OPPENHEIMER: Mr. Los Alamos, I hum, I hum the mouse

formula and I do no harm.

POET: *"He" talks with a shadow; "I" disappears.*

Sky, Detail

https://soundcloud.com/kingdomcomeradioshow/sky-detail-ii

FOUR

All these incredible antlers mark the edges

When I say the forest has a face I mean what one sees when one says a forest has a face. Something moving at the speed of digital, something else at playback. Hence the masquerade of motion and expanse, one where I can open the window (that makes it all real) where a bolt of geese intones. You cannot see the splices. You cannot see the exact moments of starts and dissolves. I have hidden these beneath a bedding of leaves in order to make the record seem more like a ghosting of birds.

ghosting *n*. 1: phenomenon measured in bandwidths or waves; *see e.g.* red shift, blue; 2: theory that matter (dark) exists without mass; 3: a kind of schema perceived, especially in twilight; this in reverse.

Traces of Lake, a Herd (for J)

When I say the lake reflects below
and for you, I mean ungulate shed

on the lakeshore. I mean chorus,
the way a jinx of trees makes the lake-body,

elk as phrase.

Are they thirsty in the next world?
Are they gazing up?

Inside the whir, soft rush of planets,
wheels of snow turn all around them.

Fancy legs, fancy feet.

Lacuna where a buck exhales
the translucent structure of antlers.

Elk-thought weighting
an iridescent belt of cold.

There are clothes we fill and then
the shed-pile knits a somber tower.

Let down your hair, you say, and I do.
Gesture for cascade, a waterfall, the rush

into dissolve, a pool of lake.
If I say your plane lands, it lands,

spingle-spangle on the runway.

You're here, late, in the kitchen.
Your shoulders, your midnight arms.

Outside us, moves we can't make.
Herds scatter in staggered rays.

No perceivable end.

Stag, Emblem, Anthem

In a fall of bone-letter confetti, shinbone,
anklebone, someone's Dodge pickup

blinkering down the mountain while on
the windshield needles, double columns,

pentameters, a billow of Bentley's 3-D micrographs,

zero visibility across the canyon.
In the horizontal blind of a whiteout,

the radio lowing *I'm so lonesome*
(I could cry). Forlorn country where

I imagine collision as a theory.
Radiant shivers of deer by the road.

Hank's resound, *That midnight train is whining low*
in glassy static and somewhere a bead on.

The bullet's trajectory set, a hammer-slam,
pow, that sound, *crack*, like a match strike,

echo plunged into the contents of a body.

The brief opening of sight
in the shatter of skull or heart.

Three bucks taken and now taking shape
on the bier of a flatbed I approach,

downshifting, slowed in the lane.
Kill limit. Triptych.

I name it.

Thicket with Dress and Lung

See how the numbers stamped on the belly of this pill
correspond to letters that make up the words UNREAL DEER?
A woman, Kitty, draws back. She can hear the ocean sigh
inside a glass of water. What goes on to say says *I went down
armed.* A statement, its image correlative: cold in sleet-sheets,
head contours. Elk or deer atop a knoll. If I am curator, a
jigger of gin, shot of Bombay in the bomb bay. If I am curator,
an I undressing, red dress, a lung.

Lit City with Fox, et cetera (for R)

In the lit city, boy on a field,
the black/white of a soccer ball.

Snow just beginning to fall, geometries
of dazzle, a mother calling, *come in*.

Between this world and another, tail,

a switch, the woodland hullabaloo,
copper cape of a fox, extravagant other.

Lucky, says the boy, he catches the sight,
chain link encircling the scene, metal

links glinting *man, beast, man, beast,*

the lavender dusk, rose-lit, so that
the field makes a sight, faux galley

for the sudden flesh marvel, fox,
the umbral-flat of it pulled behind.

Fox as trot, tracks by an edge line.
Fox as shape of its skull, bellyful

of bird, plait of ribs, a heart.

Fox as flare, little bellow,
a *stay awhile* until the shape

slips, noiseless, into underbrush.
Fox City, says the boy, name

for the miracle below ground.

Illumined whole of a hollow,
mica stars, roots and tubers wrapped

around the animal riot.
Bark-marks. Breath-marks.

Cry-marks.
Red wattage of fox rising along a score.

I Touch the Grass, I Find a Hank Song

Tell me the dream again, its animal patches, stumplands and fields. In the damn flyway a preacher machine. Says *what makes you sleep*, says *harm*. And moonlight's no-word through branches. Has seen too much coming, threadbare, sad, pine, a cowbell, goat with bowed head.

Is it place departing, *baby, that's knocksville,* someone out on the lawn long after gone. Is it a Hank song.

One and countless, a body's sorrow.

I give him dress clothes. I give him a belt, buckle, a Cadillac bench seat, another morning for morphine's eidolic rabbit gunning. I lay it all out, listen: *chuck-will's-widow* singsongs a nightjar. Sound enough for an earhole called Radio Tears Reign.

Documentary with Oppenheimer and Mezzotint

Out of the carport, ribbon of bats/*Cyan*

An eek leaks/*undersong*

Let the record reflect/*(un)singing*

Dense interior/*an echolalia*

I'm the good witness/*I gather the clamor*

Bats making purple-black chinks/*pattern recognition*

Patchwork/*crosshatch*

Exposure with Owls

Soft piping of an owl, two owlets, in the pine.

Low violet above, impromptu,

a mare's-tail formation at the edge of sight.

Look, look, I say, and they do.

My body, my skin. My spine.

Swoop, a swooping, but mum.

As if nothing is there.

My self.

Movement of blood through arteries.

Dark-gorgeous atmosphere.

Grass, Detail

https://soundcloud.com/kingdomcomeradioshow/grass-detail

Notes

ONE

Twilight amphitheater: Einstein's dramaturge credit is based on his claim that the primary human emotion is the mystery of existence. The phrase "Every cut is a lie" belongs to Werner Herzog.

Oppenheimer Drive is titled for a street named for Julius Robert and Kitty (Puening) Oppenheimer in Los Alamos, New Mexico.

The pedal bone, or coffin bone, is the principal bone enclosed within the hoof of a horse.

A "Bambi Bucket" is a slurry or water bucket used by helicopters to combat forest fires.

Neutrinos, also called ghost particles, are weakly interacting subatomic particles that pass through all matter, including Earth, virtually undetected.

Rye whiskey, a cry is borrowed from "Rye Whiskey," a traditional American folk song.

Gerardus 't Hooft is a Nobel prizewinning theoretical physicist credited with elucidating the quantum structure of electroweak interactions.

Italicized lines "I am he/she, am I?" and "I am the bird, am I?" are variations on two lines by Muriel Rukeyser.

Canna flowers bloomed around the most contaminated areas in Hiroshima ten days after the bombing.

Cryptochrome are flavoproteins sensitive to blue light and found in the eyes of birds, allowing them to sense magnetic fields for migration navigation. One of the recently discovered effects of nuclear detonations is the alteration of the planet's magnetic fields.

The italicized phrase "Where eyes meet" belongs to Issui Yoshida.

One day after the bombing of Nagasaki, Yōsuke Yamahata, a 28-year-old photographer for the Japanese News and Information Bureau, was dispatched to photograph the devastation. Over a period of 12 hours, he took around a hundred exposures. His photographs are now considered the most complete documentation of the aftermath of the bombing. Yamahata was diagnosed with terminal cancer in 1965, likely a result of his exposure to radiation in Nagasaki. The number part of "rhapsody of teeth 0.0-1.3.3/3.1.3" represents the dental formula for deer, i.e., number and placement of canines, incisors, premolars.

Among remains, teeth last longer than any other part, including bone.

Deer, Detail can be heard here:
https://soundcloud.com/kingdomcomeradioshow/deer-detail

TWO

Wolf Project with Fear of Wolves was inspired in part by Cai Guo-Qiang's *Head On*, an installation of ninety-nine manufactured wolves barreling into a glass wall. They push on relentlessly, crashing with full force against the transparent barrier. About the piece Guo-Qiang states, "I wanted to portray the universal human tragedy resulting from this blind urge to press forward, the way we try to attain our goals without compromise."

Big Sky Is a Country refers to an Associated Press, June 17, 2011 article: "A Montana woman photographing a bald eagle in a spruce tree near her house also made a picture of what was left of its prey—a fawn carcass dangling from a power line."

Documentary with Sea, a Weeping (Fukushima, 2011):
Following a major earthquake, a 15-meter tsunami disabled
the power supply and cooling of three Fukushima Daiichi
reactors, causing a nuclear accident on March 11, 2011. All
three cores largely melted in the first three days.
"Brilliant light, boom" is a translation of the Japanese
pika-don, a word integrated into Japanese vocabulary after the
bombings.
The italicized line "there may never be a snake" belongs to
Mary Jo Bang.
In recent years, the Sea of Japan has experienced extreme
jellyfish population explosions, likely a result of global
warming.
Documentary with Kitty and Fire Show: The Shelter Show
was a Los Alamos radio broadcast established during the
Manhattan Project.
Sky Piece can be heard here:
https://soundcloud.com/kingdomcomeradioshow/sky-piece

THREE

The phrase "the big hand of death" belongs to Muriel
Rukeyser.
Jackrabbit and Black Hole: Oppenheimer was haunted,
weeks prior to the detonation of the first atomic test at Trinity
Site, with the fear that a nuclear chain reaction might ignite
the atmosphere.
Sonnet for Kitty: The last two lines are Oppenheimer's own.
How Mercurial, the Water Tower (after Meret Oppenheim):
Oppenheimer's mother, Ella Friedman, an artist, was born
without a right hand and wore a prosthesis and white glove
throughout her life. The image is Meret Oppenheim's *Glove*;

see copyright and licensing credit below.

Remains, Mountains, Rivers (Japan, 1960): The title plays on Du Fu's "After the Kingdom, mountains and rivers remain." The italicized line "I feel no worse tonight than last" is Oppenheimer's, a statement made while visiting Japan in 1960. Beethoven's String Quartet in C Minor was played at Oppenheimer's funeral in 1967.

I Am Oppenheimer: Italicized lines are taken from poems by the Japanese poet Issui Yoshida (translations by Yuki Tanaka and Mary Jo Bang.)

Sky, Detail can be heard here:
https://soundcloud.com/kingdomcomeradioshow/sky-detail-ii

FOUR

Stag, Emblem, Anthem: the italicized lines "I'm so lonesome (I could cry)" and "That midnight train is whining low" belong to Hank Williams.

"3-D Bentley's" refers to the work of Wilson Bentley, who captured stunning photomicrographs of more than 5,000 snowflakes during his lifetime.

Grass, Detail can be heard here:
https://soundcloud.com/kingdomcomeradioshow/grass-detail

The following sources were consulted for biographical information in these poems: *J. Robert Oppenheimer, A Life*, Graham Pais, Oxford University Press, 2006; *The Making of the Atomic Bomb*, Richard Rhodes, Simon and Schuster, 1986; *Brotherhood of the Bomb*, Greg Herken, Henry Holt and Company, 2002; *The House at Ottawi Bridge*, Peggy Pond Church, University of New Mexico Press, 1959.

Acknowledgments

Thanks to the editors of the following publications where some of these poems have appeared, often in earlier versions. *Booth9*, *Catch-up*, *Gulf Coast*, *Sonora Review*, *Interrupture*, *The Drunken Boat*, *West Branch Wired*, University of Arizona Poetry Center, Gatherings, Poetry Society of America (poetrysociety.org), *Evening Will Come*, *The Volta*, *Perihelion Review*, *Privacy Policy*, *The Poetry of Surveillance* (anthology, ed. Andrew Ridker). Thanks also to All Along Press and The University of Arizona Poetry Center for producing "I Touch the Grass, I Find a Hank Song" and "Traces of Lake, a Herd (for J)" (the latter in earlier version) as broadsides. "Deer, Detail"; "Sky Piece"; "Grass, Detail"; "Broadcast for Kitty with Sparkle and Fade"; "Remains, Mountains, Rivers (Japan, 1960)" and "Thicket with Dress and Lung" appear in *textsound.org*, Issue 19.

For their careful readings of these poems at various times, thanks to Sheila Black, Stacey Richter, Nancy White, Barbara Cully, Joan Houlihan, Karen Brennan and John Iurino.

Special thanks to Mary Jo Bang.

Thank you Peter Covino, Sarah Kruse, and everyone at Barrow Street for production of this book.

To John, Lucia and Renz: big love and gratitude for your patience, love, and support.

Joni Wallace is the author of *Blinking Ephemeral Valentine* (Four Way Books, 2011), selected for the Levis Prize by Mary Jo Bang, and a chapbook, *Red Shift* (Kore Press, 2001). Her poetry has been featured on the website for the Poetry Society of America and appears in journals and anthologies such as *Boston Review, Conduit, Connotations Press, Gulf Coast, Crazyhorse, West Branch Wired, The Volta,* and *Privacy Policy, The Poetry of Surveillance* (ed. Andrew Ridker). Joni currently lives with her family in Tucson, Arizona, where she teaches at the University of Arizona Poetry Center.

Photo: Britta Van Vranken

BARROW STREET POETRY

Kingdom Come Radio Show
Joni Wallace (2016)

In Which I Play the Run Away
Rochelle Hurt (2016)

The Dear Remote Nearness of You
Danielle Legros Georges (2016)

Detainee
Miguel Murphy (2016)

Our Emotions Get Carried Away Beyond Us
Danielle Cadena Deulen (2015)

Radioland
LesleyWheeler (2015)

Tributary
Kevin McLellan (2015)

Horse Medicine
Doug Anderson (2015)

This Version of Earth
Soraya Shalforoosh (2014)

Unions
Alfred Corn (2014)

O, Heart
Claudia Keelan (2014)

Last Psalm at Sea Level
Meg Day (2014)

Vestigial
Page Hill Starzinger (2013)

You Have to Laugh: New + Selected Poems
Mairéad Byrne (2013)

Wreck Me
Sally Ball (2013)

Blight, Blight, Blight, Ray of Hope
Frank Montesonti (2012)

Self-evident
Scott Hightower (2012)

Emblem
Richard Hoffman (2011)

Mechanical Fireflies
Doug Ramspeck (2011)

Warranty in Zulu
Matthew Gavin Frank (2010)

Heterotopia
Lesley Wheeler (2010)

This Noisy Egg
Nicole Walker (2010)

Black Leapt In
Chris Forhan (2009)

Boy with Flowers
Ely Shipley (2008)

Gold Star Road
Richard Hoffman (2007)

Hidden Sequel
Stan Sanvel Rubin (2006)

Annus Mirabilis
Sally Ball (2005)

A Hat on the Bed
Christine Scanlon (2004)

Hiatus
Evelyn Reilly (2004)

3.14159+
Lois Hirshkowitz (2004)

Selah
Joshua Corey (2003)